Welcome to School!

Dona Herweck Rice

Get Ready

wake up

eat

brush

wash

dress

Go to School

walk

bike

bus

car

van

Greetings

say hello

wave

smile

high five

fist bump

Morning Meeting

calendar

weather

share

sing

pledge

People at School

teacher

student

class

principal

custodian

Places at School

classroom

office

library

cafeteria

playground

School Furniture

board

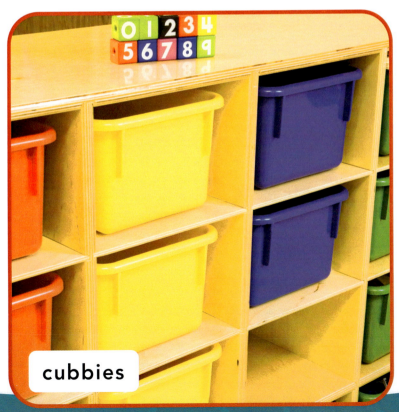

cubbies

School Supplies

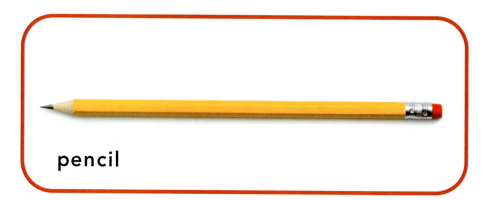

pencil

crayons

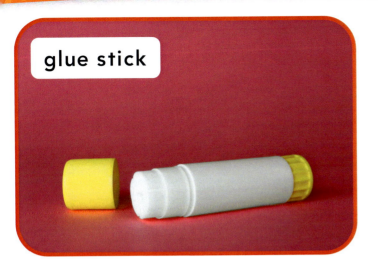

glue stick

scissors

paper

Recess

play

swing

kick

run

friends

School Rules

line up

listen

raise hands

walk

be kind

Go Home

clean up

pack up

say goodbye

leave

read together

Consultant
Janessa Lang, M.A. Ed.
Elementary Teacher, Los Angeles

Publishing Credits
Rachelle Cracchiolo, M.S.Ed., *Publisher*
Emily R. Smith, M.A.Ed., *SVP of Content Development*
Véronique Bos, *VP of Creative*
Fabiola Sepulveda, *Art Director*

Image Credits: ; p.9 (bottom) Getty Images/Jamie Grill; p.13 (middle) Getty Images/Richard Hutchings; p.14 (bottom) Alamy/Simon Turner ; p.22 (top) Getty Images/Ariel Skelley; all other images from iStock, Shutterstock, or in the public domain

Library of Congress Control Number available upon request.

This book may not be reproduced or distributed in any way without prior written consent from the publisher.

5482 Argosy Avenue
Huntington Beach, CA 92649
www.tcmpub.com
ISBN ISBN 979-8-3309-0481-5
© 2025 Teacher Created Materials, Inc.